Ramon Lull's

BOOK OF
KNIGHTHOOD
&

and the anonymous

ORDENE DE
CHEVALERIE

Ramon Lull's
BOOK OF KNIGHTHOOD & CHIVALRY

Translated by William Caxton
Rendered into modern English by Brian R. Price

ISBN: 1-891448-42-0

The Chivalry Bookshelf
1-866-268-1495
http://www.chivalrybookshelf.com

© 2001 Brian R. Price

Table of Contents

Introduction

"The knowlege of [chivalry] should be put into books, that the art is known and read in such a manner as other sciences have been read, that the sons of knights learn first the knowledge that pertains to the order of chivalry after they have been squires."

Ramon Lull stands as one of the true chivalric champions, a man who not only lived by his convictions, but one who, in commiting them to words, preserved something of the knightly ideal outside of the romantic sphere and ensured their survival to our present day. The Book of Knighthood and Chivalry lives today as a key text for anyone interested in what it meant or means to be a knight—in many places it has become, as Ramon intended, the book to be read and digested for squires and other students of chivalry.

Chivalry, as Dr. Maurice Keen so ably noted, is a problematic term. It can mean a variety of things, based on context; it can mean a collection of knights, "the chivalry," it can mean a deed of prowess—as is so often recorded in the celebratory chronicles or an act that earns renown for its expression of one of the other chivalric virtues—courtesy, courage, largesse, loyalty, franchise, verity, humility, fidelity, faith. Chivalry is many things, yet it is not defined by whatever virtues happen to appeal. As a collection of virtues, qualities and duties, the components of chivalric renown remain surprisingly consistent across secular and romantic literature, diverting only in the sharply religious treatises.

In this book, Ramon Lull and the anonymous author of the Ordene de Chevalerie offer the student of chivalric lore two clear, and closely related expressions of knightly virtue. Both stand as cornerstones of chivalric literature, key books whose depth of expression invite continual review and contemplation.

Today, interest in these chivalric handbooks comes from several quarters; students of medieval romance or knighthood, philosophy or theology; practitioners of Western martial arts in search of a philosophical base to frame their arts; and modern tournament society combatants or members of chivalric orders.

For the former groups, an accessible edition of these works will hopefully provide a clear articulation of key concepts traceable through literature, philosophy, chronicles and theology.

For the latter, the handbooks represent something more. Not only are they the clearest articulation of something that represents a "chivalric code" popularized in film and modern literature, but they also provided clear distillations of Western idealism that provide the force supporting a whole range of medieval and quasi-medieval communities.

For those who pursue knighthood as a method of improving character and teaching values to successive generations of children and youth, these works are invaluable. They describe in detail what is expected of a knight, the virtues that earn renown, a knight's duties, and somthing of the myth underlying chivalry's backward-looking origins. Together they provide a framework and a training manual for young knights and squires.

The Ordene de Chevalerie

Of the two, the Ordene de Chevalerie is of the earlier date, an extremely influential verse romancelet whose symbolism of the knighting ceremony and the knight's accoutrement can be traced both into Lull and into Charny, as well as into the mainstream of romantic literature for the next two centuries.

The Ordene tells the tale of a knight—Sir Hugh de Tabarie—who has been captured by Saladin and his ransom set. Unfortunately he cannot pay this amount, so Saladin agrees to set him free so long as he is knighted by Hugh, so impressed has he been with the conduct of Christian knights. Hugh details the symbolism surrounding each element of the knight's equipment, interpretations that echo throughout two centuries of romantic literature and chivalric handbooks.

No one knows who penned the Ordene, and while its content is symbolically apocryphal, countless thousands of knights did go through very similar ceremonies, and it retains its power eight centuries later, in the twenty-first century, as knights are made in various chivalric orders and reenactment societies.

Ramon Lull's Book of Knighthood and Chivalry

About Ramon Lull we know a great deal more, although this book represents an extremely small portion of his written works; indeed he is best known not as a knight but for his sometimes heretical ideas formally styled "Lullism."

Ramon was born on the island of Majorica in the early 1230s, the son of a wealthy merchant who settled on the island after James I of Aragon took the island from the Moors in 1229. Ramon was educated at court and eventually won the post of the island's seneschal from James II, whose patronage continued; indeed it was James who secured his release after his imprisoned captured at the siege of Almeria in 1309. He married Blanca Picany in 1257 and sired two children. There are many lively accounts of Ramon's early life at court. He was reputed to be an active tourneyer, a seeker of feminine attention, a poet and colorful court personality interested in the livliest colors that life offered to a young, intelligent and rich member of the Aragonese court.

In 1263 or 4 he seems to have undergone a series of visions that induced him to renounce his former life completely. He divested himself of goods and family, donating his worldly wealth. Guided in his spiritual endeavors by the continued patronage of James II and the Dominican Master-General Ramon de Penyafort, Lull studied for nine years, steeping himself in Arabic, Greek and other languages in preparation for journeys of the body and spirit that would take him throughout the Christian world.

In 1274, atop Mount Randa near Palma, he seems to have had a spiritual revelation that enabled him to crystallize his thoughts on Divinity into the Ars Magna, his first exposition of what became known as "Lullism." Ramon traveled Europe, seeking audiences with the Pope, teaching at Saint-Denis, and continuing to write prolificly in Latin, Arabic and Catalan. Eventually he wrote more than three hundred and fifty works, including encyclopedias and tracts of many sorts. Most, however, dealt with his unique spiritualism that polarized thought in ecclesiastic circles.

It is now known, unfortunately, into which period of Ramon's life the Book of Knighthood and Chivalry belongs. Suppositions have placed it in his early life, but the high spiritual tone seems to support a later date following his conversion. Given that a continued press of crusading was advocated by Lull in his writings in the late 1280s and the lack of any mention seems to place the work into one of his less-prostelyzing periods, but probably an early one, when he remained close to his chivalric roots, perhaps in the late 1260s.

Although dating of the manuscript is difficult, it is clear that the specific virtues he espouses are the same list as may be found in the romances; indeed as Dr. Keen has pointed out, there is evidence that some of his passages were influenced directly by the prose romance Lancelot.

Future scholarship remains to be done, but it is clear that at least the senitments put forth by Ramon in his landmark work were if not directly influential, then at least emblematic of the chivalric ideals as expressed not only in romance literature, but in martial treatises as well.

I am more than proud to make this fine work available in modern English. It has for too long been inaccessible; the earlier monographs we began to offer in 1994 have proven exceptionally popular, and with the growing convergence between students of chivalric lore, reenactors, Western martial artists, and medievalists the time seems right to release this new version. I hope it brings much pleasurable contemplation and provokes thought along what it meant and what it means to be a knight.

Brian R. Price
Union City, California

The hermit instructs a squire from Ramon Lull's Book of Knighthood & Chivalry, British Library, MS Royal 14 E11 fo 338. By Permission from of the British Library.

¶ Here after foloweth the mater
and tenour of this said Booke .
And the Fyrst chappter saith how
the good Heremyte deuysed to the
Esquyer the Rule & ordre of chy
ualrye

Contrey ther was
in which it happed that
a wyse knyght whiche
longe had mayntened
the ordre of chyualrye
And that by the force
& noblesse of his hyghe
courage and wysedom
and in auenturyng his body had mayntened warres justes & tornoyes/& in many
batailles and had many noble vyctoryes &
glorious/& by cause he salve & thouzt in his
corage yf he myzt not long lyue/as he whiche
by long tyme had ben by cours of nature
nyghe vnto his ende/came to hym an he-
remytage / For nature faylled in hym by
age / And hadde no power ne vertu to vse

a iij

Here Begins to table of this
present book entitled

"THE BOOK OF THE ORDER OF CHIVALRY AND KNIGHTHOOD"

Ramon Lull

Unto the personage and divine glory of God who is Lord and Sovereign King about and over all things celestial and worldly, we begin this book of the order of chivalry to show the significance of God the Prince Almighty, who has dominion over the seven planets, who makes their celestial courses, has the power and dominion in governing and ordaining the terrestrial and earthly. And likewise over the kings, princes, and great lords who ought to have power and dominion over the knights. And the knights who ought to have power and dominion over the masses of people.

This book contains eight chapters

1. The first chapter tells how a knight who is now a hermit devised to the squire the rules and order of chivalry
2. The second chapter tells of the beginning of chivalry
3. The third chapter tells of the office of chivalry
4. The fourth chapter tells of the examination that ought to be made of the squire when he would enter the order of chivalry
5. The fifth chapter tells in what manner the squire ought to receive chivalry
6. The sixth chapter tells of the significance of the arms that belong to a knight
7. The seventh chapter tells of the customs that pertain to a knight
8. The eighth chapter tells of the honor that ought to be done to a knight

And thus ends the table of the book of chivalry

Book One

Hereafter follows the matter and tenor of this said Book. The first chapter says how the good hermit devised to the squire the Rule and Order of chivalry

The noble Hermit Knight

A country was there in which it happened that there was a wise knight who had long maintained the order of chivalry. By the force of nobility and his high courage, his wisdom and in adventuring, his body had been maintained in wars, jousts and tourneys. In many battles had he been [in] which there were many noble victories. Because he saw and thought in his heart that he might not live long, he who for a long time had been by course of nature nigh unto his end, caused himself to seek hermitage.

For nature failed him by age, and he had neither the power nor virtue to use arms as he was wont to do, so that his heritage and all his riches he left to his children, and made his habitation or dwelling place in a great wood that had water and great trees that bore fruit of diverse types. Thus he fled the world because of the feebleness of his body in which he was taken by old age. And that he dishonored not that which in honorable things and [in] adventures had long been time-honored, the same knight thought on death, contemplating departure from this world and into the other, and of the right redoubtable sentence of our Lord in which he behooved to come to the day of Judgment.

In one part of the same woods was a fair meadow in which was a tree well-laden and charged with fruit, upon which the knight of the forest lived. And under the same tree was a fountain fair and clear that quenched and moistened the entire meadow. In that same place was the knight accustomed to come every day to pray and to adore God Almighty, to whom he rendered thanks for the honors he had done in the world all the days of his life.

Of the Squire who was Lost
on his way to receive Knighthood

It happened that at the beginning of a strong winter that a very noble king, wise and full of good customs, sent for many nobles because he was to hold a great court. By the great renown of his court, it happened that a squire moved himself to go there with the intention that there he should be made a knight.

Thus he went all alone, riding upon his palfrey. It happened that for the travel he had done he fell asleep upon his horse. In the meanwhile he rode too long while sleeping, and his palfrey issued out of his way and entered into the forest of the Hermit-knight. And so long went he, that he came to the fountain at the same time that the knight who dwelled in the wood to do his penance was coming there and praying to God, in order to despise the vanities of the world as he was accustomed to do every day.

The Meeting

When the squire came, the hermit left his prayer and sat in the meadow in the shadow of a tree and began to read a little book that he had in his lap. And when the palfrey came to the fountain and began to drink, and the squire who slept alone felt that his horse moved not, he lightly awoke. And then to him came the knight who was very old and had a great beard, long hair and a feeble gown worn and broken from over-long wearing. And by the penance that he daily made was discolored and very lean. By the tears that he had wept were his eyes wasted and had the regard and countenance of a very holy life. Each marveled at the other, for the knight who had been so long in his hermitage had seen no man since he had left the world. And the squire marveled at him strongly, as he had since he had come to that place.

Coming down from his palfrey, the squire sat in the grass next to the hermit. The knight received him wisely; regarding him with care. Both regarded each other for a long time before they spoke. The knight knew that the squire would not speak first out of his reverence. Thus, the knight spoke first and said, "Fair friend, what is your intent and why have you come hither to this place?"

"Sir", said he, "the Renown is spread to far countries that a noble king has commanded a general Court, at which he was to be made knight. And after adoubing and making other new knights, he made his intention to make foreign knights [also] known. And therefore I go to this court to be adoubed knight. But my travel and journey has been long, and while I dozed my palfrey went out of her right way, and has brought me to this place."

When the knight heard the [squire] speak of knighthood and chivalry, he remembered those days of fame and that which pertains to a knight. He cast out a great sigh and entered into great thought remembering the honor in which chivalry had been maintained.

While the knight thus thought, the squire asked him why he was so pensive, and the knight answered, "Fair son, my thought is of the Order of Knighthood or Chivalry, and of the greatness in which a knight is beheld in maintaining the greatness of the honor of chivalry."

Then the squire prayed to the knight that he would say to him the order and manner wherefore he ought to better honor and keep himself in high worship as he ought to after the ordinances of God.

The Hermit says that knights need to know the rules and orders of chivalry, and that none should make knights who are incapable of intructing them in the same

"Now son," said the knight, "knowest thou not what is the rule and order of knighthood? I marvel at how darest thou demand chivalry or knighthood until the time that you know the order. For no knight may love the order and not know the ordinances that pertain to his order; he must know the difficulties that he does against his order in not knowing. No knight ought to make knights unless he himself who makes the knight and can show them the order and customs of chivalry."

The Squire answers the knight in humility and asks for instruction

The knight said these words to the squire who had demanded knighthood, yet knew nothing of chivalry. The squire answered and said to the knight, "Sir, if it be your pleasure, I beseech you, that you will say and tell to me the order of chivalry, for well it seems to me and I think that I should learn it, for the great desire that I have hereto. And after my power I shall follow it, if it please you to teach and show it to me."

The Rule and Order of Chivalry
is in this little book

"Friend," said the knight, "the Rule and the order of chivalry is written in this little book that I hold here in my hands, in which I read, and am busy with sometimes, to the end that it makes me remember or think on the grace and bounty that God has given and done to me in this world, because I am honored and maintained with all my power in the order of chivalry. For likewise as chivalry gives to a knight all that to him appertains, in likewise a knight ought to give all his forces to honor chivalry."

Then the knight delivered to the squire this little book.

The squire marvels at the book,
and finds understanding

And when he had read therein, he understood that the knight only, among a thousand persons, is chosen worthy to have a more noble office than all the thousand. And he also understood about the little book, the Rule and Order of Chivalry, which he had for a long time desired. Without it he knew neither the nobility of the order nor the honor in which our lord God has set all those who are in the Order of Chivalry.

The hermit charges the squire to make and copy the book, and to return to the Hermit and tell him of the new knights

The knight said, "Fair son, I am an old, feeble man who may not live much longer for you. And there-fore this little book that is made for the devotion, loyalty and ordinances that a knight ought to have in holding his order, you shall bear it with you to Court as you go, and show it to all those who would be knights. And when you have been newly dubbed a knight, you shall return to your country, coming again to this place, and let me have the knowledge of who they are who have been made new knights, and shall thus be obeisant to the doctrine of chivalry."

The squire goes to court, and presents the book to the king and to the other noblemen who are to be knighted

Then the knight gave to the squire his blessing and took his leave of him. The squire took the book very devoutly, and after he mounted upon his palfrey went forth hastily to court. When he arrived there, he presented the book wisely and ordinately to the noble king, offering it to every nobleman who would be in the order of chivalry, that he might have a copy of the book, and that he might see and learn of the order of knighthood and chivalry.

Book Two

The second chapter is of
the beginning of chivalry or knighthood

hen Charity, Loyalty, Truth, Justice and Verity fell in the world, then began Cruelty, Injury, Disloyalty and Falseness. And therefore there was error and trouble in the world in which God had created man with the intention that man be known and loved, doubted, served and honored. In the beginning, when to the world came wickedness, Justice returned by dread in the honor in which she was wont to be, and therefore all the people were divided by the thousands. Of each thousand was chosen a man most loyal, most strong, and of noble courage; better educated and mannered than all the others. He was inquired and searched for, he who was best and was covenably most fair, most courageous, and most able to sustain trials, and the most able to serve mankind.

The Horse was chosen because it was the most noble and the derivation of the words chivalry and knight

It was found that the horse was the most noble and most covenable to serve man, and because of that, among all beasts, men chose the horse and gave him to this same man. For after the horse which is called cheval in French that the man named chevalier which is knight in English. Thus the most noble man is given the most noble beast.

It behooves after this that there should be chosen all the amours such as are most noble and most covenable to battle; in order to defend the man from death. And these armours were given and appropriated to the knight.

He who would enter into the Order of Chivalry should think on these beginnings

Then he who would enter the order of chivalry should think on the noble beginnings of chivalry for it behooves he who would be [a] knight—that is his nobility, his courage, and his good customs accord to the beginning of chivalry. For if it were not so, he should be contrary to his order and to his beginnings. And therefore it is not a covenable thing that the order of chivalry receive enemies in honor, nor those who are contrary to the beginnings. Love and dread be against hate and wickedness. And therefore it behooves the knight that by nobility and courage and by noble custom and bounty, and by the honor so great and so high that he is made by his election; by his horse and by his arms be loved and redoubted by the people; and that by his love he recovers charity and learning, and by deeds recovers Verity and Justice.

Why men are of more noble courage than are women, and why they are more rigorous, and why men have greater merit towards good

In as much as a man has more wit and understanding and is of a stronger nature than a woman (for if he were not more powerful and different to be better than the woman it should ensure that bounty and strength of nature were countrary to bounty of courage and good works), then a man by his nature is more appareled to have noble courage and to be better than the woman. In likewise he is much more inclined to be vigorous than a woman, for if it were not thus he should not be worthy because he had a greater merit to be good, more than a woman.

Because chivalry bestows honor on the Knight, they are more bound to be virtuous towards God and towards the people

Beware you squires who would enter into the order of chivalry what you will do, for if you are a knight you receive honor and servitude that must be given unto the friends of chivalry. In so much as you have more noble beginnings and have more honor, you are also bound to be good and agreeable to God and to the people. And if you are wicked, you are an enemy of chivalry and contrary to His commandments and honors. So very high and very noble is the order of chivalry that knights are made of the most noble persons, and should be given to them the most noble beast, and the most noble armours. But it behooves him and it must be that he is made lord over many men, for in seignority there is much nobility and in servitude much order.

Neither horse, nor armour, nor election makes a knight worthy. He is a part of the three estate system where some work, some pray, and some fight; all to Gods will

Then if you take the order of knighthood and are a vile and wicked man you will do great injury to all your subjects and to your fellows who are good; for by the vileness in you if you are wicked you should be put under a serf or bondsman. And by the nobility of knights who are good it should be judged that you are not worthy to be a knight though you are called one. Neither election, nor horse, nor armour suffices to the high honor which belongs to a knight. It is behooven that he be given a squire and servant who may take heed of his horse, and it is also behooven that the common people labor on the land to bring fruit and goods whereof the knight and his beasts have their living. And that the knight rests himself and sojourns after his nobility and pursues sport upon his horse to hunt or in other matters that please him. And that he eases himself and delights in things over which his men have pained and worked.

The clerks study doctrine and knowledge, so that they may know God and love him and His works, to the end that they give doctrine to the lay people and bestow by good examples to know, love, serve and honor God our glorious lord, to the end that they may ordinately do these things they follow and show in schools. Then by this do the Clerks by honest lives, good examples, and knowledge have gotten order and offices inclining the people to devotion and good lives. And in likewise the

knights by nobility of courage and by force of arms maintain the order of chivalry. And have the same order, to
the end that they incline the small people, by dread by
which one doubts wrongdoing to the other.

The education of squires

The knowledge and school of chivalry is such that
the knight makes his son learn in his youth to ride,
for if he does not learn it in his youth he shall never learn
it in old age. And it behooves that the son of a knight
in the time that he is a squire should take on the keeping of a horse. It behooves him also to serve, and that he
be the first subject of the lord, for otherwise he will not
know the nobility of lordship when he [himself] should
become a knight. And therefore every man who would
come to knighthood should learn, in his youth, to carve at
the table, to serve, to arm and to adoube a knight; for in
likewise as a maid will learn how to sew in order to be a
tailor or or to be a carpenter that can sew or hew. Likewise it behooves that a noble man who loves the order of
chivalry and would be a knight would first have a master
who is a knight, for thus it is a dis-covenable thing that a
squire should learn the order and nobility of chivalry from
any other man than a knight. So very high and honored
is the order of chivalry that a squire should suffer himself not only to learn to keep horse and learn to serve a
knight, that he go with him to tourneys and to battles;
but it is necessary also that he beholds the school of the
Order of Knighthood.

There should be Schools of Chivalry: chivalry should be taught like any of the other sciences

The knowlege of [chivalry] should be put into books, that the art is known and read in such a manner as other sciences have been read, that the sons of knights learn first the knowledge that pertains to the order of chivalry after they have been squires. They should ride through diverse countries with the knights and there should be no error in the clerks and in the knights under whom they study. By the clerks they should have devotion and love of God, and by the knights they should gain doubt to do wrong, to treason, and the barating of one another. Then as the clerks and masters and doctrine gone to the schools to learn, so should the squires go to learn the chivalric sciences. There have been many sciences that are written of and ordered in doctrine. Great wrong is done to the order of knighthood that it is not a written science and read in schools, like the other sciences. Therefore he who made this book beseeches the noble king and all the noble companies of great knights in this court assembled in the honor of chivalry, of the wrong that is done so that it may be amended and satisfaction done.

Book Three

Of the Office that pertains to a knight

The Knight and his Office

The office of a knight is the end and the beginning. If a knight uses not his office he is contrary to his order and to the beginnings of chivalry as was said before. By that contrarity he is not a knight; how is it that be bears the name? For such a knight is more vile than the smith or the carpenter, who does their office after they owe and have learned. The office of a knight is to maintain and defend the holy Catholic faith, by which God the Father sent his son into the world to take human flesh and the glorious Virgin our lady Saint Mary. And to honor and multiply the faith suffered in this world by many works, and despite this, [met] an anguished death. Likewise did our lord God choose the clerks to maintain the holy Catholic faith with scripture and reasons against miscreants and non-believers. God of glory chose the knights because by force of arms they vanquished miscreants who labored daily to destroy the holy church and such knights God holds as friends, honored in this world, and in that other, when they keep and maintain the faith by which we intend to be saved. The knight who has no faith and uses no faith is contrary to those who maintain it as is the intention of a man to whom God has given reason and uses it to the contrary. Then he who has faith and [does] contrary to faith will be saved, but he does so against himself. For his will accords to miscreance, which is contrary to faith and salvation. By which miscreance a man is judged to torments infernal and perdurable.

That knights and clerks are both divinely noble, but the clerks more so by their better devotion to God, though the knights and clerks ought to work together

Many there have been who have offices which God has given them in this world that He should be served and honored, but the most noble and the most honorable offices have been those of clerks and of knights. And therefore the greatest friendship in this world should be between clerks and knights. Thus as clerks are not ordained by their clergy that they not be against the order of chivalry also are knights not to be contrary to the clerks who are bound and maintained to love them. The order is not given to man that he should love his order only but he ought to love the other orders as well. For to love one order and to hate the other is not to love. For God has made no order that is contrary to any other. Thus as the religious who loves so much his own order that he is the enemy of another, he follows not the teachings of the roles of the orders. For if a knight loved the order of chivalry and destroys some other order it should seem that the order would be contrary to God, which may not be, since He established the idea of order.

So very noble is the order of chivalry that every knight ought to be a governor of a great country or land. But there have been too many knights, and the land may not suffice to signify that one ought to be the lord of all things. The Emperor ought to be a knight and lord of knights because the Emperor has under him kings who are knights; to the end that they aid and help maintain the order of chivalry. And the kings ought to have under them dukes, earls, viscounts, and other lords. And under the barons ought to be knights, who ought to govern the ordinances of the barons who are in the high degree of chivalry named before, to show excellence, leadership, the power and the wisdom of our lord glorious God who is the only God in trinity, who can and may govern all things. Therefore it is not covenable that a knight should allow himself to govern all the people of this world, for if one knight alone might do so, the leadership, power and wisdom of God should not be so well signified. And therefore to govern all the people in the world, God willing, that there are many knights whom he is the only governor, as it was said at the beginning. These kings and princes who make provosts and bailiffs of persons other than knights have done against the office of chivalry, for if the king is more worthy to have leadership over the people than any other man who [is of] such an honorable office, and by that honor receives his order, he has nobility of heart and noblesse of courage; he is less inclined to do a villainous deed than another man.

The knight must maintain and defend his worldly lord and the knights should be judges if they were more learned in wisdom

The office of a knight is to maintain and defend the worldly lord, for a king who has no barons has no power to maintain righteousness in his men without aid and help. Then if any men do against his commandment of his king or prince it is behooven that the knights aid their lord, who is but a man only as another. He is an evil knight who sooner helps another man that would put down his lord from the seignory that he ought to have upon him, and he follows not the office by which he is called a knight.

By the knights ought to be maintained and kept justice, for in likewise as the judges have the office to judge, likewise do the knights have the office to keep them from violence in exercising the deeds of justice. It must be that chivalry and clergy are assembled together in such manner that knights and clergy should be friends; so that by science they were sufficient to be judges. No offices should be so covenable to judge as chivalry, for he who may best behold justice is more covenable to be a judge than any other.

Knights must undertake such sports as to make themselves strong in prowess, yet not forget their duties

Knights ought to take coursers to joust and to go to tourneys, hold an open table, to hunt harts, bears, and other wild beasts, for in doing these things the knights exercise themselves to arms and thus maintain the order of knighthood. It is wickedness to love the customs to which a knight practices but to despise the order to which he belongs.

All of these things aforesaid pertain to a knight as touching his body; in likewise do Justice, Wisdom, Charity, Loyalty, Verity, Humility, Strength, Hope, Swiftness and all other virtues touch the soul.

The knight must also practice such things as will exercise the soul, as well as his body

And therefore the knight who uses the things that pertain to the order of chivalry as touching his body and has none of the virtues that pertain to chivalry as touching the soul is not the friend of the order of knighthood. For if it were thus, that he made separation of the virtues above-said, saying that they pertain not to the soul and to the order of chivalry together, it should signify that the body and chivalry were both together contrary to the soul and to these virtues.

And that is false.

The knight must maintain his land

The office of a knight is to maintain the land, for because of dread of the common people have of the knights, they labor and cultivate the earth, for fear, lest they should be destroyed. And by their dread of the knights they redoubt the kings, princes and lords, by whom they have their power. But the wicked knight who aids not his earthly lord and natural country against another prince is a knight without office, and belief; which is against faith.

A knight must aid his lord; his lord must foster chivalry in himself ere he destroy it in his subjects

Then if such a knight follows the office of chivalry in destroying himself and does not aid his lord, such a knight and his order should do wrong to that knight who fights unto death for Justice and to maintain and defend his lord. There is no office that He made but that it may be defeated, for if that which is made mighty may not be defeated, that would be a thing similar to God (who may not be defeated or destroyed). As the office is made and ordained of God, it is maintained by those who love the order of chivalry. The wicked knight who loves not the order of chivalry defeats the knight in himself. But the evil king or prince who defeats in himself the order of chivalry defeats it not only in himself but he defeats it also in the knights who have been put under him. By the wicked example of their lord, they engage in disloyal flattery so that they are loved by him.

And by this reason the wicked princes are not only contrary to the order and office of chivalry to their own persons, but they are also contrary to those who have been subsumed under them, in whom they defeat the order of chivalry.

If to cast a knight out of chivalry is great cruelty and great wickedness, it is a greater fault to cast many out of chivalry. A bad prince or baron has in his court or in his company wicked knights; false traitors who never admonish him that he does wrong; he berates, treasons, and extorts his subjects. The good prince, by the strength of noble courage, and by the great love and loyalty that he has to chivalry, surmounts these vices, vanquishing and destroying them, therefore he destroys chivalry not.

Of such great strength and courage and great nobility is he, the friend of chivalry, when he takes vengeance on such enemies who would take him and pluck him away from the honor of chivalry, and corrupt his noble courage.

Chivalry is more in accord with courage than in strength of the body

If chivalry were stronger in the body than is strength of courage, the order of chivalry should be more in accord with the body than with the soul. If it were so, the body should be more noble than the soul, and that is openly false. Then nobility of courage may not be vanquished from man, nor surmounted, nor all of these men who have been what she is in her right strength. And when a body is lightly taken and vanquished of another, it is obvious that courage of man is more strong and noble than the body.

A knight who is in battle with his lord, who for lack of courage flees from battle, when he should give aid, because he more redoubts or fears the torment or peril more than his courage uses not the office of chivalry. Neither is he the servant nor obedient to other honors, but it is against the order of chivalry, which was bygone by nobility and courage. If the lesser nobility of courage should better accord to the order of chivalry than to the greater one of the soul, until chivalry should accord sloth of heart and cowardice against hardiness and strength of courage. And if it were thus, hardiness and strength of courage should disordain the order of chivalry.

That is openly false.

Therefore a noble knight who loves chivalry less has less aid from his fellows, is less in arms and has less to defend. So much more is he behooved to enforce himself to have the office of a knight by hardiness of a strong courage and of noble appearance against those who are contrary to chivalry. And if he dies in the maintenance of chivalry then he acquires chivalry in that place where he may better love and serve it. For chivalry abides not so agreeably in any place as in nobility of courage. And no man may honor and love chivalry more, and may not do more than to die for love and for the honor of the order of chivalry.

Knights must possess wit and discretion

Chivalry and hardiness may not accord without wit and discretion If it were thus that foolishness and ignorance should be contrary to the order of chivalry, this would be impossible. This impossibility is openly signified by the knight who has great love to the order of chivalry. In likewise as chivalry by nobility of courage has made knights to have hardiness so they could doubt neither peril nor death, that you might honor chivalry. The order of chivalry makes you love and honor the order of chivalry against the disordinance and default than to follow the order of chivalry by foolishness and ignorance without listening.

The knight must maintain and defend women, and respect and defend those less powerful than he

The office of a knight is to maintain and defend women, widows and orphans, men diseased; and those who are neither powerful nor strong. For as custom and reason is that the greatest and most mighty helps the feeble and the lesser, and that they should have recourse to the great. Right so is the order of chivalry because the great, honorable and mighty must succor and aid those who are under them, those less mighty and less honorable than he. Then as it is so that to do wrong and to force women and widows, who have need of aid, and orphans who have need of governance, and to rob and destroy the feeble who have need of strength, and to take away from them that which is given to them. These things may not accord to the order of chivalry, for this is wickedness, cruelty, and tyranny.

The knight must seek both justice and mercy

And the knight who instead of these vices is full of virtues is dignified and worthy to have the order of chivalry. Likewise as God has given even to the weak man for to see to work, right so has he given even to a sinner, to the end that he is aware of his sins. And in likewise as God has given to the knight a heart, to the end that he is hardy by his nobility. So ought he to have mercy in his heart. And that his courage be inclined to the works of misiacord and piety. That is to wit: to help and to aid those who are weeping, who require the knights aid and mercy and who in the knights have their hope. Then knights who have eyes which cannot see the feeble and weak, have not the heart nor the might by which they may record the deeds to be in the order of chivalry. If chivalry, which is so very much an honorable office, were to rob and destroy the poor people and the unmighty, and then do wrong to the good women and widows, who have no way to defend themselves, then that office is not virtuous, but vicious.

The knight must possess such riches as to support his office, lest he be forced to robbery

The office of a knight is to have a castle and horse for to keep the ways and to defend those who labor on the lands and in the earth and they ought have towns and cities to hold right to the people. And to assemble in that place men of many diverse crafts, which are necessary to the ordaining of this world and to keep and maintain the life of the man and of the woman.

Then as knights who maintain their office are so much praised, they should be lords of towns, castles, cities and of many people. If they intend to destroy castles, cities and towns, burn houses, hew down trees, slay beasts and rob on the highways were to the office of chivalry, it should be disordinance to chivalry. For if it were so, chivalry would not be so well ordained, for then the good ordinances and its contrary would be one thing; and that may not be.

The knight must search for thieves, robbers and oppose wickedness

The office of a knight is also to search for thieves, robbers and other wicked folks, to make them be punished, for in likewise as the axe is made to hew and destroy the evil trees in likewise the office of a knight [was] established to punish the trespassers and delinquents.

He must not be a robber

If a knight is a robber, wicked and a traitor, and that it is true that robbers and traitors ought to be taken and delivered to death by the knights, then late the knight so attached to the wicked conditions takes Justice and Right of himself and uses his office as he ought to do of others. And if he will not use himself in his office like he should upon others, it follows that he should love the order of chivalry better than he loves himself. And therefore a knight who is a robber and a thief ought to be taken and delivered unto death by other knights. And every knight who sustains and suffers a knight to be a robber and a thief, in so doing he uses not his office. For if he used it in that manner, he should then go against his office. Therefore all false men and traitors ought to be destroyed; those are not true knights. An evil knight is closer to hell than are you or I. They are less knights than you or I, I who am a clerk. Then every knight [who is] a traitor and robber is more near to that art than to me who am no knight nor of thine office as he who sustained and is such by default. And if that same evil grieves more than me, wherefore then excuses the punishing of such a man who is contrary and an enemy of chivalry; they be not knights.

He must not steal, because more than goods, he steals from the high honor of chivalry

First, a knight who is a thief does greater theft to the high honor of chivalry in as much as he does that which takes away from the name knight without cause, as he who takes away or steals money or other things. To steal or take away honor is to give evil fame and renown. And to blame that thing which is worthy to have praising and honor, for honor is worth more than gold or silver without comparison. It is said that it is a greater fault to steal or take away chivalry than to steal money or other things. For if it were to the contrary, it should follow that money and other things should have more value than honor. Secondly, if any traitor who slays his lord or lays with his wife or betrays his castle were named a knight, what name should that man have that to honor and defend his lord in arms? Thirdly, if a knight, being a traitor, is born out of fault, what fault he then make of which he is reprieved and punished since his lord punishes him not for treason? And if his lord maintains not the order of chivalry in punishing a traitor knight, in whom shall he maintain it? And if he destroys not this traitor, what thing shall he destroy?

He must not put his wife, or his possessions, in the keeping of untrustworthy men

Little knows he and evil keeps him who commands his sheep into the keeping of the wolf, who puts his fair wife into the keeping of a young traitor knight, and his strong castle delivered into a covetous knight's keeping. And if such a man who thus foolishly delivers to keep his things, how should he keep well the things of other men? Is there no knight who would gladly keep his wife from a traitor knight? Certainly I know this to be true. Also, is there no knight covetous and robbing, who has never fain to steal? Certainly no such knight, evil and wicked, might not be brought again, nor redressed to the order of chivalry.

He must have a good horse and complete harness

To have a harness fair and good and to know the keeping of himself, to take heed of his horse is the office of a knight; that is to say, that a knight should welcome those who have come to do his work as a good master, to the end that they whom he has commissioned to do or to make things, he could reprieve of their faults. If to have no harness and no harness were the office of a knight, it should seem that which that is, and that which is not were the office of a knight. But to be and not to be, should be things contrary. Wherefore a knight without harness may not be and neither ought he be made knight.

Perjury

There is a commandment in our law that no Christian man shall be perjured; also that a false oath ought to be reprieved in the order of chivalry. And he who has perjured himself is not worthy to be a knight. If a squire is of vile courage and would be a knight he will destroy the order for which he asks.

And because God and Chivalry concord together, it behooves that false swearing and untruth should not be in those who maintain the order of chivalry.

Lechery and Humility

And if lechery and Justice accord together, chivalry that accords Justice should accord do lechery; and if chivalry and lechery accorded, Chastity which is contrary to lechery should be against the honor of chivalry; were it so that to maintain lechery knights were honored in maintaining chivalry. It has been seen that lechery and Justice are contrary, and that chivalry is ordained to maintain Justice. The knight should be just and totally contrary to lechery, wherefore the order of knighthood was first established. And if Justice and Humility were contrary, chivalry which accorded him not Justice should be contrary to Humility. And if he accords himself to pride, he should be contrary to humility.

Humility

If a knight who is proud maintains chivalry, he corrupts his order which was begun by Justice and Humility to sustain the humble against the proud. For if it were so those who are now knights should not be in that order. But all the knights now injurious and proud, full of wickedness, are not worthy of chivalry; but ought to be reputed to be for naught. Where then are Humility and Justice? What have they done? What do they serve? And if Justice and Peace were contrary, chivalry that accorded Justice should be contrary to Peace, and by those who love wars, thefts, and robbery should be knights. And to the contrary; they who pacify and accord the good people and who flee the tribulations and wickedness of the world should be evil and wicked knights.

A rail against knights who fail to practice justice or preserve the right

But the High Emperor God who sees and knows all that is contrary and otherwise [to His will]. For the felons and injurious are all contrary to chivalry, and to all honor—I ask those who were first knights who accorded Peace and Justice—and pacified by Justice and force and strength of arms. Likewise in the time which chivalry began was the office of chivalry to pacify and accord the people by force of arms. The injurious knights and warriors who are now maintained and ordained into the order of chivalry, in many manners owe and in many ways may a knight use the office of knighthood. But because we have to speak of many things, we pass over as lightly as we may; and also at the request of the right courteous squire, veritably loyal and well studied in all courtesy and honor, who for so long has desired the rule and order of chivalry, we have begun this book for the love of him and for his desire and will to accomplish for him the purpose to briefly speak in this book because he will shortly be adoubed and made a new knight.

Book Four

Of the examination of the Squire who will enter the order of chivalry or knighthood

The examiner should be of high repute, and should seek to raise knighthood only those who are worthy

To examine a squire who would enter into the order of chivalry it behooves him well he will examine him to be a knight. And that next after God he love above all things chivalry or knighthood. For there have been some knights who love better great numbers of evil knights rather than a little number of good knights. And not withstanding Chivalry has no regard to the multitude of numbers, but loves only they who are full of noblesse of courage, of good learning and it has before been said.

Therefore if the examiner loves more the multitude of knights than the nobility of chivalry, he [is] not covenable nor worthy to be an examiner and it should be necessary that he is examined of the wrong that he has done to the order of chivalry.

The Squire should love and fear God, for if he does not then he does not have the noble habit required of a knight

First the examiner asks of the squire who will be knight if he loves and dreads God, for without the love and dread of God no man is worthy to enter the order of chivalry. And dread makes him fear the difficulties by which chivalry takes dishonor. When it happens that the squire who does not dread God is made knight, he takes the honor in receiving chivalry and receives dishonor. Therefore a squire without love and dread of God is neither deigned nor worthy to be a knight; for he loves not that which he intends to destroy by his evil nature. And he who makes a knight of vile courage by favor does against his order and charges his conscience. Such is not noblesse of courage in the mouth. For every mouth says not the truth; nor seeks it not in honorable clothing; for under many a fair habit has often been vile courage full of baseness and wickedness. Neither seek for it in the horse, for he be not the answer. Nor seek for it in the fair garments or harness, for within fair garments is often wickedness and the heart of a coward. Then if all you find is nobility of courage, ask it of Faith, Hope, Charity, Justice, Strength, Temperance, Loyalty and other noble virtues. For in them is the nobility of courage; by them is defeated the heart of a noble knight from wickedness, from treachery, and from the enemies of chivalry.

The knight must be of an appropriate age, that he understands his duty

Ovenable age pertains to a new knight; for if the squire who would be a knight is too young, if he is made a knight in his infancy, he may not remember that which he promised to the order of chivalry, when he shall need to remember it. And if the squire who will be a knight is vile and does villany and injury to chivalry, which is maintained by strong men and fighters and is defiled by cowards and the feint of heart, the unmighty, those overcome, and by those who flee.

Likewise by virtue and measure abide in the middle of two extremes, that is to wit pride and vice, right so a man ought to be made knight and be nourished in competent age and always [be] virtuous by right measure. For if it were not thus, it should follow that the contrariness between chivalry and measure, and if it were so, virtue and chivalry should be contrary. And in the squire who is negligent and slow to be a knight, wherefore wilt you then be in the order of knighthood or chivalry? If by beauty of fashion or by a body fair and well adorned or by fair hair, by regard or to hold the mirror in the hand and by other jolities, should a squire be dubbed a knight of villains and of people of little lineage, low and vile, making them knights. And if you made them, the lineage [of chivalry] you should dishonor and err. And the nobility that God has given greater to men than to women and bring it to vileness.

Because of vanity, women should not be made knights

By the things before said you might choose women to be knights, they who often have the mirror in the hand, by which [action] you should diminish and make low the order of chivalry in so much that only vile women or only villainy of heart might come to be put into the right high honor of the order of chivalry.

Knights should be taken from the natural nobility, because they require nobility of the soul more than strength of the body

Peerage and chivalry accord together, for peerage is nothing but honor anciently accustomed. And chivalry is an order that has endured since the time in which it was begun unto this present time. And because peerage and chivalry acccord together, if you make a knight who is not of the peerage you make chivalry contrary to peerage, and by the same reason, he who you make a knight is contrary to peerage and to chivalry then you may not have so much or who has other similar vices should not be accorded the order of chivalry. If chivalry might receive those who are against the order, it should follow that in chivalry ordinance and disordinance would be one proper thing, and since chivalry is known as the order of Valor, every squire ought to be examined before he should be made knight.

Book Five

In what manner a squire ought to be received in the order of chivalry

When a squire should be made knight

At the beginning, it behooves a squire entering the order of chivalry to confess of his difficulties that he has done against God and ought to receive chivalry with the intention that he should serve our God, who is glorious. And if he is cleansed of sin he ought to receive his savior, for to make and adoube a knight it should only be the day of some great feast; Christmas, Easter, Whitsontide or on such solemn days; because by the honor of the feast assemble many people in that place where the squire ought to be adoubed knight & God ought to be adored and prayed that he give the squire grace to learn well thereafter the Order of Chivalry.

Fast and Vigil

The squire ought to fast on the vigil of the same feast in honor of the saint of whom the feast is made. That day he ought to go to the church to pray to God. He ought to stay awake all night and say his prayers and ought to hear the word of God and things touching the deeds of chivalry for if he otherwise plays and is ribauld, hearing speak of putery and sin he should begin them by dishonoring chivalry.

After the Knighting Day, A Sermon

On the morning after the feast in which he has been adoubed it behooves him to hear a mass to be sung solemnly and the squire ought to come thereafter and offer to the present which holds the place of our Lord the honor of whom he must oblige and submit himself to keep the honor of chivalry with all of his power. In that same day ought to be made a sermon in which should be recounted and declared the twelve articles upon which is founded the Catholic faith; the ten commandments and the seven sacraments of the Holy Church and other things that pertain to the faith. And the squire ought to diligently take heed and retain these things to be then kept in mind [with regard to] the office of chivalry touching the things that pertain to the faith.

The Twelve Articles of Faith

The twelve articles are such: to believe in one God only; that is the first and behooves him to believe that the Father, the Son, and the Holy Ghost are only one God in three persons, without end and without beginning, which makes up the fourth article. To believe that God is the creator and maker of all things is the fifth; the sixth is to believe that God is the redeemer, that is to say that he has redeemed or brought again the human lineage from the pains of Hell to which it was judged by Adam and Eve, our first father and mother. The seventh is to believe that God gave glory to those who are in heaven.

These seven articles pertain to deity and the other following pertain to humanity

That the son of God took our Lady Saint Mary, is the first of the seven articles following.

⟨ To believe that Jesus Christ was conceived of the Holy Ghost who Saint Gabriel the archangel gave Salvation to Our Lady.

⟨ The second and third are to believe that He has been crucified and died to save us.

⟨ The fourth is to believe that his soul descended into Hell to deliver his friends; that is to wit Adam and Abraham and other prophets who believed in His holy coming.

⟨ The fifth is to believe that he raised from the dead to life.

⟨ The sixth is to believe that he stayed up in heaven to Ascension day.

⟨ The seventh is to believe that Jesus Christ shall come at the day of judgment when all shall arise and shall be judged the good and the evil and shall give to every man pain or glory that each deserved in this transitory world. In behooves to all good Christian men to believe these articles which bore witness to God and His works, for without these articles no man may be saved.

The Ten Commandments

The commandments of God which He gave to Moses upon the mount of Sinai are ten. The first is that you shall adore, love and serve only one God. Nor should you be perjured. Hallow and sanctify the Sunday; Honor thy mother and father; Be thou not a murderer or commit homicide; do no theft nor fornication; Nor bear false witness; Nor covet the wife of thy neighbor; Nor have thou envy of the goods of thy neighbor. To all knights is behooven to know the ten commandments that God has given.

The Seven Sacraments

The sacraments of the Holy Church are seven. They are to wit: baptism; confirmation; the sacrament of the altar; the order of marriage; penance and unction. By these seven sacraments we hope all to be saved. And a knight is bound by his oath to honor and accomplish these seven sacraments. And therefore it pertains that every knight should know his office well and the things to which he is bound since he had received the order of knighthood. And all these things before said, and of others that pertain to chivalry. The preacher ought to make mention of these preachings in the presence of the squire, who ought to pray devoutly to God to give him His grace and His blessing by which he may be a good knight all the days of his life from then on.

The knight who adoubes the squire must be virtuous
He cannot give what he does not have

When the preacher has said all that pertains to his office, then must the Prince or Baron who will make the squire & adoube him a knight, should have in himself virtue and the order of chivalry, for if the knight who makes knights is not virtuous, how may he give that which he has not? Such a knight is of worse condition than are the plants, for the plants have the power to give their nature to one another, and of beasts and fowls it is also a similar thing. Such a knight is evil and false who disordinately and willfully multiplies his order, for he does wrong and villainy to chivalry. He will do that which is not a covenable thing to do and that by which he ought to honor chivalry he defeats and blames. Then if by default such a knight, it sometimes happens, [whom] the squire receives chivalry from is not so much aided nor maintained of the grace of our Lord, nor of virtue, nor of chivalry as he should be if he were made by a good and loyal knight. And therefore such a squire is a fool and all others similarly who receive from such a knight the order of chivalry. The squire ought to kneel before the altar and lift up to God his eyes corporeal and spiritual, and his hands to heaven, and the knight ought to gird him in sign of Chastity, Justice, and of Charity with his sword. The knight ought to kiss the squire and give to him a palm because by that he remembers that which he receives and promises and of the great charge in which he is obliged and bound and of the great honor that he receives with the order of chivalry.

After his knighting, he ought to ride among the people; the knowledge of this pledge keeps him from evil

And after the spiritual knight (who is the priest) and the terrestrial knight have done what pertains to their office as touching and making of a new knight, the new knight ought to ride through the town and show himself to the people to the end that all men know and see that he is a newly made knight, and that he is bound to maintain and defend the high honor of chivalry. For he shall have great refrainment from doing evil, for by his shame that he shall have of the people who know of his chivalry, he shall withdraw himself so much the more than to act against the order of chivalry.

And he ought to give a great feast, and give gifts, showing largesse according to his means

On that same day it behooves him to make a great feast and to give fair gifts and great dinners; to joust and to sport and to do other things that pertain to the order of chivalry. To give to Kings of Armes and to heralds as it is accustomed of ancient; and the lord who made the new knight ought to give the new knight a present or gift also; and the new knight ought to give to him and to others that same day, for whom so receives so great a gift as is the order of chivalry honors not his order if he gives not after the power he has to give. All these things and many others I will not recount because of shortness of time pertaining to chivalry.

Book Six

Of the Significance
of the Arms of a Knight

Wherein the Hermit speaks of the sword, helmet, and other equipment necessary for the knight, and the things that are symbolized by these things

That which the priest invests him when he sings the mass have some significance which concords with the office. And the office of priesthood and chivalry are of great concordance. Therefore the order of chivalry requires all that is necessary to a knight, as touching the use of office, to have some importance, by which is signified the nobility of chivalry and [of] his order.

The Knights Sword
In the Semblance of a Cross, it symbolizes Justice

Unto a knight is given a sword, which is made in the semblance of a cross to signify [that] our lord God vanquished in the cross the death of human lineage, to which he was judged for the sins of our first father Adam. Likewise a knight owes to vanquish and destroy the enemies of the cross by the sword, for chivalry is to maintain Justice. And therefore is the sword made to cut on both sides, to signify that the knight ought with the sword to maintain chivalry and Justice.

The Knights Spear or Lance
Signifying Truth

To the knight is given a spear to signify truth, for truth is a thing right and even. And that truth ought to go before falseness. The iron or head of the spear signifies strength, which truth ought to have above falseness. And the pennon signifies that truth shows faith to all, and has neither dread nor fear of falseness or treachery. And Verité is sustained of Hope and also of other things which have been signified by the spear of the knight.

The Knights Helmet
Represents Fear or Shame

The hat of steel or iron is given to the knight to signify shamefastness, for a knight without fear of shame may not be obedient to the order of chivalry. As fear of shame causes a man to be ashamed and makes him cast down his eyes against the earth, likewise the hat of iron defends a man, enabling him to look upwards on high, but also makes him look towards the ground and thus is in the middle between the things high and low. For it covers the head of a man, which is the most high and principal member of the body; fear of shame defends the knight who has the most high and noble office—that is the office of a clerk—that he inclines not to bow to villainous deeds and that the noblesse of his courage neither abandons him nor gives him to feuding, wickedness nor to any evil teaching.

The Knights Hauberk
Signifies strength against Vices

The hauberk signifies a castle and fortress against vices and faults; for likewise as a castle or fortress is closed all about, in likewise a hauberk is firm and closed in all places to the end that it gives significance to a noble knight that his courage ought not enter into treason, nor to any vice.

The Knights Chauces or Leg Harness
That he should hold himself securely to his ways

Chauces of iron or the legharness are given to a knight to keep and hide surely his legs and feet from peril, to signify that a knight with iron ought to hold himself upon the ways [of chivalry]; that is understood with the sword, spear and mace. And other garments of iron to take the malefactors and punish them.

The Knights Spurs
Signify Diligence and Swiftness

The spurs are given to a knight to signify diligence and swiftness, because with these two things every knight may maintain his order in the high honor that belongs to it. For likewise as with the spurs does he prick his horse causing it to hasten to reign, right so does diligence hasten the knight to do his duty and make him procure the harness and the dispenses that are necessary to a knight, to the end that a man is not surprised to be taken suddenly.

The Knights Gorget
Signifies Obedience to his Lord and to Chivalry

The gorget is given to signify obedience, for any knight who is not obedient to his lord nor to the order of chivalry has dishonored his lord and issues out of the order. And right so as the gorget runs around or goes about the neck of the knight, because it should be defended from strokes and wounds, in likewise makes obedience of a knight to be within the order of chivalry, to the end that neither treason nor pride, nor any other vice corrupts the oath that the knight has made to his lord and chivalry.

The Knights Mace
Strength and Courage

The mace is given to the knights to signify strength and courage, for in likewise as a mace or pollaxe is strong against all arms and smites all parts, so force of strength in courage defends a knight from all vices, enforcing virtue and good customs by which knights maintain the order of chivalry in the honor which it is due and which pertains to it.

The Knights Misiacorde
To trust in God, more than his own Strength

A misiacorde or knife with a cross is given to a knight to signify that if his other armours fail him, he has recourse to the misiacorde or dagger. Or if he is so close to his enemy that he may not smite him with his spear or his sword then he may join him and surmount him [using] the misiacorde or knife. And because the weapon which is named misiacorde shows a knight that he ought not to trust all in his arms nor his strength but he ought to affirm and trust in God and to join to him by right good works and much hope, that he ought to have in him, and that by the help and aid of God he vanquishes his enemies and those who are contrary to the order of chivalry.

The Shield
Defense of his Prince

The shield is given to the knight to signify the office of a knight, for likewise as a knight puts his shield in between himself and his enemy, right so the knight is in the middle between the prince and the people. And as the stroke that falls upon the shield saves the knight, right so the knight ought to call himself out and present his body to his lord when his lord is in peril of being hurt or taken.

The Gauntlets
Keeps him from injury and from touching evil

Gauntlets are given to a knight to the end that he puts his hands therein to be sure and to receive the strokes if his other defenses fail him. And thus as a knight with his gauntlets handles more surely his spear and his sword. The significance of the gauntlets is to lift up high his hand. Right so he ought to lift them up in thanks to God for the victory that he has had. By the gauntlets is also signified that he ought not lift up his hand in making false oath, nor handle any evil, nor touch anything foul or dishonest.

The Saddle
Surety of Courage

The saddle in which the knight sits when he rides signifies surety of courage, the charge and the great burden of chivalry. For likewise by the saddle is he sure upon his horse, right so surety of courage causes a knight to be in the forefront of the battle, which the surety of adventure—the friend of chivalry—will aid him. And by surety are recognized many cowards, vaunters and many vain semblences which make men cowards for seeming hardy or strong of courage. And by that are many men refrained that they dare not pass to the fore in that place, where noble courage and strength ought to be, and pass above the course of a knight valiant and hardy.

And by the saddle is also signified the charge of a knight. For the saddle likewise as we have said holds the knight firm upon his horse, so that he may not fall or be moved lightly, but if he wills it. And therefore the saddle which is so great signifies the charge of chivalry, that the knight ought to in no way move for light things, and if it behooves him to move, he ought to have courage, nobility and hardiness against his enemies to enhance the Order of Chivalry.

The Knights Horse
Noblesse of Courage

To a knight is given a horse, and also a courser to signify noblesse of courage. And because he is well horsed and high is why he may be seen to be free from fear. And that is the signicance that he ought to be made ready to do all that which behooves the order of chivalry more than another man would. To a horse is given a bridle. And the reigns of the bridle are given to the hands of a knight because the knight may at his own will hold the course the horse and refrain him. And this signifies that the knight ought to refrain his tongue, and hold that he speaks neither foul nor false. And it signifies that he ought to refrain his hands, that he gives not so much that he is suffrous and needy. And that he begs or asks not; nor ought he be so hardy that in his hardiness he has reason and temperance.

The Reigns
The knight should be led by chivalry and duty

And by the reigns is signified to the knight that he ought to be led overall where the order of chivalry will lead or send him. And when it shall be time of necessity to make largesse, his hands must give and dispense after that which pertains to honor, and that he be hardy, and doubt nothing of his enemies, for doubt enfeebles strength of courage. And if a knight does contrary to do all these things, and his horse keeps better the rule of chivalry than he does, to his horse is given in his head a testiere to signify that a knight ought to be bear no arms without reason, for as the head of a horse goes before the knight does, for all works without reason are vices in him. Likewise as the testier keeps and defends the head of the horse, right so reason keeps and defends a knight from blame, and from shame.

The Bardings
Signify the worldly goods necessary
To maintain the office of chivalry

The bardings are to keep and defend the horse, and they signify that a knight ought to keep his goods and his riches, because they might suffice for him to maintain the office of chivalry. For likewise as the horse is defended of the strokes or hurts but his garments, and without them he is in peril of death, likewise a knight without temporal goods may not maintain the honor of chivalry, nor may he be defended from evil perils, for poverty causes a man to think basely, falsehoods and treasons, and to that purpose says scripture, "Porptor inopiam multi delinquozant," for poverty has made many men false.

The Knights Surcoat
The hardships a knight will face
in the service of chivalry

A coat is given to a knight in significance of the great hardships that a knight must suffer to honor chivalry, for likewise as the coat is above the other garments of iron, and is in the rain and receives the strokes before the hauberk and other armours, right so is a knight chosen to sustain greater travaille than a lesser man. And all the men who are under his nobility, and in his guard ought to be when they have need to have recourse to him. And the knight ought to defend them after his power. And the knights ought rather to be taken, hurt or dead, than this happen to the men under their guard. Then as it is right and great chivalry, therefore the princes and barons in such great office travaille to keep their lands and people.

The Knights Heraldic Device
Symbolizes his renown earned, fair or foul

A token or insignia of arms is given to a knight on his shield and on the coat so that he is known in battle, and so that if allowed, if he is hardy and if he does great and fair deeds of arms; or if he is a faulty coward, or recreant; the arms are given to him because he can be blamed, vitupered, reprieved. The arms are also given to a knight to the end that he be known if he is a friend or enemy of chivalry, wherefore every knight ought to honor his device, that he is kept from blame, the blame which casts the knight and puts him out of chivalry.

The Knights Banner
Symbolizes his honor and duty to defend his lord and his land

The banner is given to the king or prince or baron and to a knight Banneret which has under him many knights, to signify that a knight ought to maintain the honor of his lord and of his land. For a knight is loved, praised and honored by the folk of worship in the realm of his lord, and if they do dishonor of the land that they be of, and of their lord, such knights are blamed more and shamed more than other men. Likewise for honor they ought to be more praised because that in them ought to be the honor of a prince, and of the knight and of the Lord. In likewise in their dishonor they ought to be more blamed. And because of their negligence, falsehood or treason are kings and princes more disheartened than any other men.

Book Seven

Of the Customs that Pertain to a Knight

Noblesse of courage has chosen a knight to be above the other men who are under him in servitude. The nobility of habits, and good nourishments pertain to a knight. For noblesse of courage may not mount the high honor of chivalry without the election of virtues and good habits. As it is, it behooves a knight that he is replenished of good customs and good teachings.

Every knight ought to know the seven virtues, which are the beginning and rote of all good habits, and are the path to celestial glory which is so easily lost. Of the seven virtues there are three theological or divine and four cardinal. The theological are Faith, Hope, and Charity; this cardinal are Justice, Prudence, Strength and Temperance.

The First Virtue
Faith

Knight without Faith may not have good habits and customs, for by Faith a man sees the spiritual God and his works, and believes in the Invisibles. And by Faith a man has Hope, Charity, and Loyalty; and is the servant of Verité and Truth. And by a fault of Faith a man should not believe that God is a man, nor fail to believe in his works and in the invisible things which a man without Faith may neither understand nor know.

Knights are accustomed by the Faith earned by travel to lands in pilgrimage, proving their strength and chivalry against the enemies of the cross, being martyrs if they die. For they fight to enhance the Holy Catholic Faith. Also by Faith are the clerks defended by the knights from wicked men, who by wicked fault rob and dishearten them as much as they may.

The Second Virtue
Hope

Hope is a virtue which very strongly pertains to the office of a knight. For by the hope that he has in God he intends to have victory in battle. By reason of the deeds that are greater in God than in his body or in his arms, he comes to surmount his enemies. By hope is enforced the courage of the knight, vanquishing negligence and cowardice. Hope makes a knight sustain and suffer trials and to be adventurous in peril, into which they put themselves often. Also, Hope makes them to suffer hunger and thirst in castles, cities and fortresses, when they have been assigned to valiantly guard and defend them as much as they are able, for if there were no hope a knight might not do his office. And also Hope is the principle instrument to the office of knighthood, as the hand of a carpenter is the principle instrument of carpentry.

The Third Virtue
Charity

knight without Charity might have cruelty and evil will. Cruelty and evil accord not with the office of chivalry, because it behooves the knight to have Charity; for if a knight does not have Charity in God and in his neighbor, how or in what way should he love God? And if had not pity in poor men, those who are mighty or are diseased? How should he have mercy on the men, captured and vanquished, who ask for mercy, who pledge not to escape, and who might not find the finances that are demanded for their deliverance? And if a knight were not charitable, how might he be in the order of chivalry? Charity is a virtue above other virtues, for she forces other vices to depart. Charity is a love of which every knight ought to have as much as is needed to maintain his office. Charity also makes a man to bear lightly the burdens of chivalry, for in likewise as a horse without feet may not bear a knight, right so a knight may not without charity sustain the great charge and burden of his Order. And by Charity may chivalry be honored and enhanced.

The Fourth Virtue
Justice

If a man without a body were a man, if a man were a thing invisible, and if he was unseen, he would not be a man. But a man is not. Likewise, if a man without Justice were a knight who used force without Justice, chivalry would be different from the chivalry we know. And how is it that a knight has the beginnings of Justice and is injurious, when to be in the order of chivalry that pertains not? For chivalry and Justice accord so strongly, that without justice chivalry may not be. For an injurious knight is an enemy of Justice; he defeats it and casts himself out of chivalry, his noble order, despising it.

The Fiftth Virtue
Prudence

The virtue is Prudence is that by which a man has knowledge of good and evil. And also by which a man has grace to be the friend of good and the enemy of evil. For Prudence is a science by which a man has knoweldge of how things came to be and as they are now. Prudence is won by mastery so that a man might eshew damages both to the body and to the spirit. And as knights are ordained to put away and destroy evil, for no men put their bodies in so many perils as knights have done. What thing is then more nececcary to the knight than the virtue of Prudence? The customs of a knight are to arm himself and to fight, but that accords not so much to the office of a knight as does the use of reason, of listening, and ordained will. For many battles have been vanquished more by mastery, by wit and industry, than my multitudes of horsemen and good armour.

And to this purpose said the valiant Judas Maccabeus to his people, when he saw his enemies, who in number sixty times more than they were, came to fight. "O my brethren," said he, "be ye not in doubt, but that God will help us at this time." For I tell you that victory lies not in great multitude, for therein lies great confusion, but by the wit and good Prudence of the said Judas Maccabeus was the said battle were his enemies vanquished and he obtained glorious victory. Then as it is so if you, knight, will accustom your son to the office of knighthood, to maintain chivalry and his noble order, make him first accustomed to reason and listening. Make him such that with all of his power he is a friend to the good and an enemy of evil. By the use of Prudence and chivalry assemble them to honor the order of chivalry.

The Sixth Virtue
Strength and Chastity

Strength is a virtue which remains and dwells in noble courage against the seven deadly sins, by which men go to hell to suffer and sustain grievous torments without end. The sins are Gluttony, Lechery, Avarice, Pride, Sloth, Envy, and Ire. Then a knight who follows such a way, goes not in the ways of nobility of heart, nor should he make these sins his habit. Gluttony causes feebleness of body by overmuch eating and drinking. In overmuch drinking, Gluttony causes Sloth and laziness of body which grieves the soul. All vices are contrary to chivalry, therefore the strong Courage of a noble knight fights with the aid of Abstinence, Prudence, and Temperance that he has against his Gluttony.

How an element of Strength — chastity — combats the sin of lechery

Lechery and chastity fight against one another, and the arms with which lechery wars on chastity are youth, beauty, heavy drinking, and eating too much meat, bright clothes, bravado, falsehood, treason, injury, and the despising of God and His glory. To doubt the pains of hell, which are for eternity, and the other things like that, chastity and strength war against lechery, and can surmount it by the remembering of His commandments, and the remembrance and understanding of the good and the glory that God has unto them who love and honor Him. Evil and pain clothe those who despise and do not believe in Him. Chastity wars and vanquishes lechery with noblesse of Courage, which will not submit to evil and foul thoughts, nor will be availed nor defouled from His high honor.

And as a knight is named chevalier because he pledges to fight and war against vices, and ought to vanquish and surmount by force of nobility and good courage, if he does not have this Strength, he is no knight, nor does he have the heart of a knight; neither does he have the arms of a knight with which he ought to fight.

How Strength combats vice and avarice

Avarice is a vice which makes noble courage descend, avail and submit to vile and foul things. By the lack of Strength and without good courage that defends them not against avarice have many submitted and been vanquished. And by that also are knights covetous and avaricious. And by their covetousness they have done many wicked and wrong things, and are then serfs who are bonded to the goods that God (whom they have abandoned) has given them.

Strength has such customs—at no time will he aid his enemy; nor fail to help a man if he asks for succour and aid. For so noble and high a thing is strength of Courage, and such great honor due it, that in times of great need during trial and peril it ought to be called upon. And aid ought to be demanded of it. Then when the knight is by avarice tempted to incline his courage thereto, which is the mother and root of all evils, and of treason, then ought to have recourse to the strength in which he will never find cowardice, nor negligence, nor feebleness, nor default of succour or aid. For with strength a man with a noble heart may vanquish all vices.

Wherefore if you have not Strength of Courage and Nobility, like the noble courage of the puissant king Alexander, who in despising avarice and covetousness always had his hands stretched forth to give until his knights, so renown was his largesse, that the soldiers of a king with whom he warred turned against him and came towards the said Alexander, confusing his covetous enemy who had been their master.

And therefore you ought to think, to the end that you do not submit to villainous works, which accord not and do not pertain to the order of chivalry. For if it pertained to it, who should deny that lechery did not pertain to a knight?

How Strength combats the sin of sloth

Sloth is a vice by which a man is a lover of wickedness and evil, drawn to hate goodness. And by the vice may be known and seen in men signs of damnation better than in any other vice. To the contrary, Strength may be better known in a man as the sign of salvation than by any other virtue. And therefore he who will overcome and surmount sloth, it behooves him to have strength in his heart, by which he vanquishes the nature of the body, which by the same Adam is inclined and appareled to do evil. A man who has sloth also has sorrow and anger, because while he knows that another man does well, and when a man does harm to himself, he who by sloth is heavy and sorrowful of that he has not more and greater. And therefore such a man is sorry both of good and evil of other men, for ire and displeasure give passion and pain to the body and to the soul.

Therefore you knights who will vanquish and surmount the same vice ought to pray for Strength, for she will reinforce your courage against sloth, remembering that if God does well by any man, therefore it follows not that he ought also to do well for He giveth all that he has nor all that he may give, nor that in so giving he takes away nothing and therefore God has given to us an example of those who labored in the vineyard. When he reprieved them who have wrought from the morning into evening that they murmured because the lord of the vinyard have as much salary and wages to them who were come to evensong time as to those who had labored all day, and said to them, that he did them no wrong, and that of his own good his might do his will.

How Strength and Humility
work together to combat pride

Pride is a vice of inequality, or to be unequal to another and not alike. For a proud man will have no peer, nor equal to him, but loves better to be alone, and not to like any other. And therefore Humility and Strength are two virtues that love equality, in that they are against pride. If you, proud knights, will vanquish your pride, assemble within your Courage, Humility, Strength. For Humility without Strength is nothing, nor may it hold against pride. And pride may not be vanquished by that. When you shall be armed and mounted upon your great horse, you should be parvenour proud. But if Strength and Humility makes you remember the reason and intention of why you are a knight, you will never be proud. And if you are proud, you shall never have the Strength in courage, by which you can cast out proud thoughts. But if you are beaten down from your horse in battle, taken and vanquished, you will not be as proud as you were before. For Strength in body has vanquished and surmounted the pride of your Courage. How is it that nobility is not a thing corporeal? Strength and Humility, which are spiritual things, are much better at casting out pride from the noblesse of Courage.

The Effects of Envy

nvy is a vice disagreeable to Justice, to Charity,
and to Largesse, things which pertain to the Order
of Chivalry. When any knight has a slothful heart and
a falling of Courage, he may not sustain nor ensue the
order of chivalry for lack of Strength, which is not in
his courage, nor has he in himself the virtues of Justice,
of Charity, nor of Largesse. Such fate is force, violence,
dishonor, and injury to chivalry. And by that is many a
knight envious of others who are well, and who are slow
to get the goods above said by strength of arms and are
full of evil courage, inclined to ready and to take away
the other mean things that are not his, and which he
was never in possession. It behooves him to think how he
makes quarrels and falsehood in order to get riches; some
times the order of chivalry is thus dishonored.

How Strength of Courage combats anger

Ire is troubled courage, a remembrance of wicked will. And by this trouble remembrance in him turns to forgetfulness, intention into ignorance, and will into retching. And as to remember, to understand, and to will are often enlightening, by which the knight may follow the way and the rule of chivalry. Who will then cast out his courage that which he does not understand? His spirit should recover strength of courage, charity, temperance and patience, all of which have dominion over the refrainment of anger. And they are to test and allegiance of the trials and passions that anger gives. Strength of Courage will surmount and join unto him benevolence, abstinence, charity, patience and Humility. And thus shall anger be surmounted. Ire and impatience and other vices are thus lessened, diminished, and the virtues, such as Justice and Wisdom, are greater. And by the greatness of Justice and Wisdom that is the order of chivalry is the greater.

The Seventh Virtue
Temperance

We have said before that the manner in which Strength ought to be held in the Courage of a knight against the seven deadly sins. And we shall hear after the virtue of Temperance. Temperance is a virtue which dwells in the middle of two vices; one is sin by overquantity and the other is sin by underquantity. Between over much and over little must be Temperance, in such reasonable quantity that it is virtue. For if there were no virtue in between the overgreat and the over little, there should be no middle—and that may not be. A knight accustomed to good customs and well trained ought to be tempered in hardiness, in eating, in drinking, in words and dispensing, and in other things similar to the same. Without temperance a knight may not maintain the order of chivalry, nor may he be a place where virtue dwells.

That the Knight should hear mass regularly, that he may better accustom himself to virtue. He should avoid superstition or divination

The custom and habit of a knight ought to be to hear mass and sermon, to adore and pray to God, and to give to the same love and dread. By that custom a knight may remember the death and filth of this world and demand of God the celestial glory and dread and doubt the pains of hell. And by that he may accustom himself to virtue and to other things that pertain to and to maintain the order of chivalry. But a knight that does the contrary and believes in divination by the flight of birds does against God who has greater faith and hope in the wind above his head and in the works that birds have done, and in the diviners, than in God and his works. And therefore such a knight is not agreeable to God, nor does he maintain the order of chivalry. Neither the carpenter nor the tailor nor any other men of craft have the power to use their office without the art and the manner that pertains to that office. And as God has given discretion and reason to a knight, by which he can use his office, and if he can live in the maintenance of the order of chivalry; if he does not then he does wrong and injury to discretion and to that which he listens and shows. And he who follows and believes in divinity and sayings that the bird flies on the right side signifies contrary to the left side. And to such things think and give affiance. Such a knight casts away noblesse of Courage, and is likened to a fool who uses neither wit nor reason. And therefore such a knight is against God.

And after right and reason he ought to be vanquished and surmounted of his enemy who uses reason and discretion against him, and who has hope in God. If it were not thus, it should follow that those who divine by the flight of birds and other things without reason and without the order of chivalry, have amongst them a concordance greater than to God; reason, discretion, hope, faith, and noble courage. And that is openly false.

Knights who give credence to the diviners who say that evil is to happen if a woman is discovered in the morning, and that he may not do a good deed of arms the day he sees the head of his wife, or any other such belief, will be laid bare and discovered by the false belief that he has. For as a judge uses his office, when he judges after custom, right so a knight uses his office when he uses reason and discretion, which are the customs of chivalry. And also as the judge who should give sentence after a witness and then gives false judgment by the flight of birds, or by barking of dogs, or by other such things which are like the same, right so does a knight do against his office if he does not that which reason and discretion show him and witness, but believes that which the birds have done by necessity. And because they are flying in the air by chance, then as it is so, by that ought to ensue reason and descretion and do after the significance that his armours represent, as we have said before, and of the things which happen by chance he ought not to make necessary by custom.

The knight should respect the common good, since for the greater good was chivalry established

To a knight pertains that he be a lover of the common wealth, for by the commonality of the people was chivalry founded and established; the common weal is greater and more necessary than the good and the special.

A knight should be Courteous, should speak well, and should have good harness and a fair horse. Chivalry is not in the horse or arms, in the power, but is rather in the knight himself, if he is committed to chivalry

To a knight pertains only to speak nobly and courteously, and to have fair harness and to be well clad, and to hold a good household and an honest house, for all these things are necessary to honor chivalry.

Courtesy and chivalry concord together, for villainous and foul words are against the order of chivalry. Privacy and acquaintance of good folk, loyal and truthful, hardy, bearing Largesse, Honesty, Humility, Piety, and the other things pertain to chivalry. And in likewise as he ought to God to compare all his nobility, right so a knight ought to compare to all that whereof chivalry may receive honor for them who are in the order. The custom and good training that a knight gives to his horse is not so much to maintain the order of chivalry as is the good custom and good training that he does to himself and to his children. For chivalry is not in the horse, nor in the arms, but is in the knight who well induces and trains his horse, and accustoms himself and his son to learn good works. And so a wicked knight, who induces and trains himself and his son to evil learning and doctrine, makes himself and his sons beasts and his horse a knight.

Book Eight

The Honor Due a Knight

od has honored the knight. And all the people honor him likewise as this book has recounted. Chivalry is an honorable office above all said offices, or orders, or estates of the world; reserving only the priesthood, which pertains to the holy sacrifice of the altar. And the Order of Chivalry is necessary as touching the government of the world. And therefore chivalry, by all of these reasons, and many others, ought to be honored by the people. If a king or prince were not corporate in chivalry, by default of that which they should not be sufficient, and that they had not in them the virtues or the honor that pertain to the order of chivalry, then they should not be worthy to be kings, nor princes, nor lords of countries; for in them chivalry ought to be honored. The knights ought then to be honored by the kings and great barons, for as the knights and the high barons are honored above the middle-people, right so the kings and the high barons above the other people ought to hold knights, chivalry and franchise according together. And to the franchise and seignory of the king or price accords to the knights, because the king is his lord; therefore it behooves him to honor the king or prince or baron and lord of a land according to the honor of a knight, in such manner that the prince or king is lord, and the knight honored. The honor of a knight pertains that he be loved for his bounty and goodness, and that he be redoubted and dreaded by his strength. And that he is prayed for his debonairity and discretion, and because he is the counselor of kings or of the prince, or of another high baron, then to set no value upon a baron because he is but a man, is to despise the things before said; for which a knight ought to be honored. Every noble baron and high lord who honors a knight and holds him in his court as his counselor and at his table honors himself. And so he who honors him in battle also honors himself. And the lord who makes a wise knight a messenger or an ambassador delivers his honor to noblesse of courage and the lord who multiplies honor in himself. And the lord who aids and maintains the knight as he does his office, and enforces his seignory, and the lord who is discreet with a knight has amity with chivalry.

To require folly to the wife of a knight, or to incline her to wickedness is not the honor of a knight. And the wife of a knight who has children of villains honors not the knight but destroys and brings to naught the amicability of the noble confraternity and the noble lineage of the knights. So too a knight who has children of villain women honors not the order of chivalry honors neither gentility nor chivalry. And as it is so then gentility and the honor of chivalry accord together in a knight and in a lady by virtue of marriage, and the contrary is the destruction of chivalry. If the men who are not knights are obliged to hold the honor of a knight, the knight is more bound and obliged to honor his body in being clad well and nobly and in being well-horsed and to have fair harness, to be good and noble, and to be served and honored of good persons without comparison, then to honor nobility of his courage by which he is in the order of chivalry. Chivalry is dishonored when Courage is disordained, and when a knight puts foul thoughts, wickedness, and treasons in himself and casts out of his courage the noble and good thoughts that pertain to the order of chivalry. The knight who dishonors himself and his peers, that is to wit another knight who is not worthy to have honor. For if he was worthy, wrong should be done to the knight who holds and does to chivalry as touching to himself and to the other knights.

Then as chivalry has its dwelling in the noble courage of a knight, no man may have such honor or dishonor in chivalry as a knight. Many are the honors and the reverences that ought to be done to a knight; and inasmuch as a knight is greater, of so much more is he charged and bound.

In this book we have spoken shortly enough of the order of chivalry. Therefore do we now here end [our talk] of the honor and law of God, our glorious Lord, and of our Lady Saint Mary, who is blessed *socula soculozum*, amen.

Caxtons Epilogue

ere ends the book of the order of chivalry. This book is translated out of the French and into the English at the request of a gentle and noble squire by me, William Caxton, dwelling at Westminster beside London in the best ways that God has suffered me and according to the copy said squire has delivered to me.

The book is not for every common man to have, but for noble gentlemen who by their virtue intend to become knights and enter into the noble order of chivalry, which in these late days (1484) has been used according to this book to be written but unfortunately forgotten in existence to chivalry; not used, honored, nor exercised as it has been in ancient times, at which time the acts of the noble knights of England who used chivalry were renowned throughout the Universal World, as for to speak for the incantation of Jesus Christ where they were ever only like Brenius and Belynus that from the Great Britain now called England unto Rome and beyond conquered many realms and lands, whose noble acts remain in the old histories of the Romans. And since the incarnation of Our Lord, behold the noble King of Britain

Arthur, with all the noble knights of the round table, whose noble acts and noble chivalry of his knights occupy so many large volumes that is a world or as a thing incredible to believe.

O ye knights of England, where is the custom and usage of noble chivalry that was used in those days? What do ye now, but to go to the banes and to play at dice? And some not well advised used not honesty and good rules again in the order of knighthood, leave this, leave this and read the noble volumes of Saint Grail of Lancelot, of Galahad, of Tristam, of Percefrost, of Percival, of Gawain, and so many more. There will you see manhood, courtesy and gentleness.

And like in the latter days of the noble acts since the conquest as in king Richard Coeur de Lyon, Edward the First, the Third, and his noble sons, Sir Robert Knolls, Sir John Hawkwood, Sir John Chandos, and Sir Walter Manny—read Froissart. And also behold that victorious and noble king Henry the Fifth, and the captains under him, his noble brethren; the Earl of Salisbury Montagu, and so many others whose names shine gloriously by the virtuous nobility and acts that they did in the honor of chivalry. Alas what do ye do but sleep and take ease, and are all disordered from chivalry. I would ask a question if I should not displease, how many knights are there in England who know the use and exercise of a knight—that is, to wit, that he knows his horse, and his horse him—that is to say, being ready at a point to have everything that belongs to a knight; a horse that is broken after his hand, his armour and harness mete and sitting so forth; et cetera? I suppose if a due search be made, there would many found who are lacking; more the pity is.

Would it please our sovereign lord that two or three times a year, or least once he would cry a joust of peace, to the end that every knight should have horse and harness, and also the use and craft of a knight, and also to tourney one against another, or two against two, and the best to have a prize, a diamond or jewel, such as should please the prince. This should cause gentlemen to resort to the ancient customs of chivalry to great fame and renown. And also to be always ready to serve their prince when he shall call them or have need. Then lately every man

who is of noble blood and intends to come to the noble order of chivalry, should read this little book, and to thereafter, in keeping with the lore and commandments herein
comprised. And then I doubt not he shall attain the order
of chivalry, et cetera. And thus this little book I present to my redoubted natural and most dread sovereign
lord king Richard (III) king of England and of France, to
the end that he commands this book to be had and read
unto other young lords, knights and gentlemen within his
realm, that the noble order of chivalry be hereafter better used and honored than it has been in late days passed.
And therein shall do a noble and virtuous deed,

And I shall pray to almighty God
For his long life and prosperous welfare;
& that he may have victory over all his enemies;
& after this short and transitory life to have everlasting
life in heaven,
where as is Joy and Blessed world without end,
Amen.

The anonymous

Ordene de Chevalerie

hat the wise speak is goodly gain,
For thereby do we win amain
Of sense, of good and courtesy:
'Tis good to haunt the company
Of him who of his ways hath heed,
And hath no keep of folly's deed.
For as in Solomon we find,
That man that is of wisdom's kind
Doth well in every deed there is;
And if at whiles he doth amiss
In whatso wise, unwittingly,
Swift pardon shall he have thereby,
Whereas he willeth pentinence.

But now I needs must draw me hence
To rhyming, and to tell in word
A tale that erewhile I have heard,
About a King of Paynemry
A great lord of days gone by;
He was full loyal Saracen
And his name hight Saladin.
Cruel he was, and did great scathe
Full many a time unto our faith,
And to our folk did mickle ill
Through pride of heart and evil will.
So on a time it fell out so
That 'gainst him to the fight did go
A Prince hight Hugh of Tabary,
Therewith was mickly company,
The Knights of Galilee, to hand;
For lord was he of that same land.
That day were great deeds done amain,
But not was our Creator fain,
He that the lord of glory hight,

That we should vanquish in the fight;
For there was taken the Prince Hugh
And let along the streets and through,
And right before Saladin,
Who greeted him in his Latin,
For well he knew it with certainty:
"Hugh, of thy taking fain am I
By Mohomet," so spake the King;
"And here I promise thee one thing,
That it behoveth thee to die
Or with great ransom thee to buy."
Then answered him the lord Sir Hugh,
"Since choice thou givest me hereto
Unto the ransom do I fall
If so be I have wherewithal."

"Yea," said the King, "then payest thou
An hundred thousand besants now."
"Ah Sir, this thing I may not do
If all my lands I sell thereto."
"Yet dost thou well." "Yea Sire and how?"
"Thou are full of hardihood enow
And full of mighty Chivalry,
Thy lords shall nought gainsay it thee,
But with thy ransom deal they should
And give thee a gift full good,
And in this wise quit shoudst thou be."

"Yet one thing would I ask of thee,
How may I get me hence away?"
Then therto did Saladin say:
"Hugh, unto me shalt thou make oath
That by thy faith and by thy troth
To come again unto this place

Without fail in a two year's space,
And they to pay thy ransom clear,
Or come back to the prison here.
Thus wise from henceforth are thou quit."
"Sir," quoth he, "have thou thank for it
And all my faith I pledge thereto."

Then craveth he a leave-to-go
That he may come to his own land.
But the King takes him by the hand
And leads him to his chamber fair
And prayeth him full sweetly there:
"Hugh," saith he, "by the faith ye owe
Unto the God whose law ye know,
Now make me wise: for sore I crave
The right road straight-away to have,
And I have will to learn aright
In wat wise one is made a Knight."
"Fair sir," he said, "this may not be,
And wherefore I will tell to thee:
The holy order of Knighthood
In thee will nowise turn to good;
For evil law thou holdest now,
Nor faith nor Baptism hast thou.
Great fool is he that undertakes
To clothe and cover o'er a jakes
With silken web, and then to think
That never more the same shall stink;
In nowise one may do the feat,
E'en so to me it were unmeet
To lay such an order upon thee,
O'er hardy were such deed to me,
For sore blame thereby I should win."
"Ha Hugh," quoth he, "nought lies herein
This is no evil deed to do
For in my prison dost thou go

And needs must do the thing I will
Howso it thee it semeth ill."
"Sir, since ye drive me to the thing
And nought avails my nay-saying,
Then riskless I the work shall earn."

Therewith he fell the King to learn
In all wise what behoved to do
With face and hair and beard thereto,
And did clothe himself right well
As to a new-made Knight befel,
And in that bath wash lithe and limb.
Then 'gan the Soudan ask of him
What these same things signify,
And answered Hugh de Tabarie:
"This bath wherein thy body is
Forsooth it signifieth this.
For e'en as infants born in sin
Stainless from out the font do win,
When they to babtism are brought,
E'en so Sir Soudan, now ye ought
To come forth free from felony,
And be fufilled of courtesy;
In honesty and in good will
And kindness shoudst thou bathe thee still
And grow beloved of all on earth."
"Beginning this fight well of worth,
By God the great," spake forth the King.

Then from that fair bath outgoing
He laid him in a full fair bed
That dearly was apparalled.
"Tell me without fail, High," he saith,
"What this same bed betokeneth."
"Sire, betokeneth now the bed
That one by Knighthood should be led

The bed of Paradise to win
Which God gives his friends therein.
For there a bed of rest there is
Made for now evil man ywis."
So on the bed a while he lay
And did on there in full fair array,
Which was of linen white of hue.
Then in his Latin said Sir Hugh:
"Sir, deem not that my word is in vain,
The web that next your skin hath lain
All white, would you do this to wit,
That Knights should ever look to it
To hold them clean, if they will well
To come their ways with God to dwell."
With scarlet gown he clad him then
And marvelled Saladin again
Wherefor the Prince bedight him so.
"Hugh," said he, "now I fain would know
What this same gown betokeneth."
Then Hugh of Tabarie answereth:
"This gown in gift is given withal
That ye may know the sum of all
And fail not more your blood to give
In serving God while ye live,
And Holy Church to fortify
That be no man it fare awry.
For all these deeds to Knights are meet
If they to God would make them sweet.
The scarlet gown betokenth this."
"Hugh," said he, "much my marvel is."

Shoes on his feet he then did no
Of loose-wrought say all brown of hue,
And spake he: "Sir, withouten fail

For thy remembrance doth avail
This foot-gear is shapen black,
That ne'er shalt thou the memory lack
Of death, and earth to lie in low,
Whence cam'st thou, wither thou dost go.
So ward ye then your eye, withal,
Lest into pride at last ye fall,
For never o'er a Knight should pride
bear sway or in his heard abide;
Of simpleness should he have heed."
"All this is good to hear indeed,"
Spake then the King, "nor grieveth me."

Then upright on his feet stands he
And girds him with a belt withal
That white is and of fashion small.
"Lo sire, this little belt doth mean
That thou thy flesh shalt hold all clean,
Thy reins and all th body of thee
And hold it ever steadfastly;
Yea, even as in virginhood
Thy body to hold clean and good,
And lechery to blame and ban.
For ever loveth knightly man
To hold his body free from stain
Lest he be shamed and honour wane.
For unclean things God hateth sore."
The King said: "Goodly is thy lore."

Two spurs thereafter did he on
His feet and word within he won:
"Sir, e'en as swift and speedily
Ad ye would wish thine horse should be,
And of good will to run aright
When ye with spurs his sides do smite,
That swiftly he may wend all wise,

And here and there as ye devise,
These spurs betokenth without doubt
(Gilt as they be all round about)
That ever heart should be in you
To serve your God your life days through.
For even thus doth every Knight
That loveth God in heart aright,
To serve him with a heart full dear."
Fain then was Saladin to hear.

Therewith he girt to him a sword
And Saladin hath asked the word
What thing betokeneth the brand.
"Sir," said he, "'tis a guard to hand
'Gainst onslaught of the Fiend to bear,
Even as now thou seest here;
The two-edged blade doeth learn thee lore
How a good Knight should ever more
Have blended right and loyalty.
Which is to say it seemeth me,
to guard the poor folk of the land
Against the rich man's heavy hand,
And feeble people to uphold
'Gainst shaming of the strong and bold;
This then is Mercy's work to win."
All this yeasateth Saladin,
Who hearkeneth well all words he said.

Thereafter set he on his head
A coif which was all shining white
And told its tokening all aright.
"Now look hereon Sir King," said he,
"E'en as this coif, as thou dost see,
Is wholly without stain or sear,
And fair and white, and clean and clear,
And sitteth now upon thine head:

So on the day of doom and dread,
Free from the great guilt we have wrought
And clear and clean from deeds of nought
Which ever hath the body done,
We then must render everyone
To God that we may win the prize
Of all delights of Paradise.
Because no tongue may tell the tale,
Ear hearken, nor a heart avail,
To think of Paradise the fair,
And what his friends God giveth there."
To all this hearkened well the King,
And afterward he asked a thing,
If aught he lacked whereof was need.

Yea sir, but dare I not the deed."
"What is it then?" "The stroke," said he.
"Why hast thou given it not to me
And told me its betokening?"
"Sir, 'tis the memory-stirring thing
Of him who hath ordained the Knight
And duly with his gear him dight
Now I will lay it not on thee,
For in thy prison here I be,
Nor ugly deed here may I do,
Lest men lay wite on me thereto;
Nor by me shall the stroke be laid;
With things so done, be thou apaid.

Yet will I show thee further-more,
And learn and tell thee o'er and o'er
Three matters weightiest to tell,
Whereof should new Knight wot full well,
And hold them all his life-days through,
If honour he would come until.
And this is first of all I wot,

That with false doom he meddle now
Nor in the place of treason bide
But light wend him thence and wide;
But if the ill he may not turn,
Thence forth away must be full yerne.
The other matter liketh well.
Never may Dame nor Damosel
Of him have any evil rede;
But if the rede of him they need
Aid them should he with all his might,
If he would fair fame aright.
For women should of worship be,
And deeds for them done mightily.

This also must thou look unto
        That rightwise abstinencto do,
And this I tell you verily
On Fridays must there fasting be,
The holy memory to bear
How Christ was smitten with the spear
Even for our redemption
And gave to Longuis pardon.
On that same day till life be past,
For the Lord's sake, then, should one fast,
But if it be for sickness sake,
Of fellowship against it make;
Of if perchance one may not,
The peace of God must then be got
By almsdeed or some otherwise.

The next and last thing I devise,
        Mass should one hear each day and all,
And offer if one have withal;
For right well offering lies ywis
That laid upon God's table is:
For there it beareth mickle might."

So hath the King heard all aright
Of all that Hugh hath told him there,
And joy he maketh great and fair.
Then stood the King upon his feet
Apparelled as was meet:
He entered straight his feast-hall fair,
And fifty admirals he found there
Who all were men of his country;
Then on his high-seat down sat he,
And Hugh before his feet sat down,
But seen had place of more renown
For the King made him sit on high.

Then spake the King: "Know verily
Because thou are a valiant man
A right fair gift for thee I can;
For this I grant thee frank and free;
When so thy folk shall taken be
In battle pitched, or in the fray
For thy love they shall go their way,
If this to crave, thou come to hand.
But if thou ride amidst my land
Without impeach fair shalt thou go
And on thy palfrey's neck thereto
Shalt lay thy helm before men's eyes
That nought of fray 'gainst thee arise.
Morever of thy taken men
Now I will give thee up to ten
If thouwilt have them whence with thee."
"Sir," said he, "of thy much mercy
Much thank and good can I: but yet
One thing I would not all forget.
Thou leadest me to seek and crave
Of good men, if I might them have,
To help me in my ransoming:

But never shall I find, O King,
A valianter than thou ywis;
Therefore give me, as right it is,
E'en that ye learned me crave of you."
King Saladin, he laughed thereto,
And spake as one well pleased would say:
"Right well hast thou begun the way,
And fifty thousand besants bright
Now will I give to thee outright;
By me thou shalt not fail herein.:"
Unto his feet then did he win
And to the lord Hugh spake he so:
"To every baron shalt thou go
And I will wend along with thee."
"Sir," said the King, "give him and me
Wherewith this mighty lord to buy."
To giving fell they presently,
The Admirals all round about,
Till all the ransom was told out
And remnant was, if all were paid,
Of thirteen thousand besants weighed;
So much they promised him, and gave.
Then would lord Hugh the free
leave have
To get him gone from Paynemry.
"Thus wise thou partest not from me,"
Said then the King, "until ye get
The remnant that is over yet
Of what behight they to be told
For all those besants of mere gold
From out my treasure we take."
Then to his treasurer he spake
To give the besants to Sir Hugh,
And take them after, as was due,
Of them who has the promise made.
Then he the besants duly weighed
And gave them to the Count Sir Hugh,

Who took them, would he, would he no.
But he to take them was unfain;
Liever were he to buy again
His folk who in the prison were
In thralldom and right heavy cheer,
In hand of barons Sarrazin.
But when thereof heard Saladin,
Then by his Mawmet strong he swore
They should be ransomed never more.
And when Hugh heard it, for his part
Great wrath he had within his heart,
But further durst not pray the King,
Since be my Mawmet swore the thing.
Nor durst he wroth him more that day.
Therewith he bade them to array,
Those ten fellows, whom he did crave
The road to their own land to have.
Yet did he tarry from the road
And there for eight days yet abode
In feast full great and all delight.
Then he let-pass craved aright
To pass therewith the foeman's land.
And Saladin gave 'neath his hand
Of his own folk great company.
Of fifty fellows there had he,
And they from Paynemry him lead
Without ill pride or evil deed,
That never had they fight or fray.
So took they then the backward way,
And to their land ride frank and free.
Therewith the Prince of Galilee
In likewise gat him home again,
But for his folk hard was his pain
That he behoved to leave behind,
Whereof no mending might be find.

So to his own land is he come
    With but those ten and hath no more.
Then shareth he the wealth good store
That thence awayward he had brought,
And unto no man giveth nought,
That wealthy wax they, each, and hail.

Fair sirs, well ended is the tale
    Amidst good people of good will;
For nought it shall be the ill,
Who nore more the sheep shall hear
By God and Paradise the dear!
For well be he his jewels tyne
Who casteth them before the swine:
They shall but tread them under feet,
And deem them neither good nor sweet.
For nothing of it should they wot
But ever understand it not,
And whoso such a tale should tell,
Down trod he should be e'en as well,
And held of nought by their un-wit.

But we who willeth learn of it,
    Two things in this tale shall find
Well worthy worship in his mind.
And this is the first, to wot aright
In what wise one is made a Knight
Such as the whole world worship shall
Whereas he wardeth one and all.
For if there were not fair Knighthood
Then Lordship were but little good:
For Holy Church it wardeth still,
And from ill doer's evil will
In right and justice keepeth all;
So this I raise what e'er befall.
Who loves it not is such as they

Who would the mass-cup steal away
That doth upon God's altar stand,
And no man now may turn their hand.
Lo, how their rightwiseness hath care
For all men good defense to bear,
For drove they not ill men away,
Good men might sure not ever a day.
Then all were Sarracens in sooth,
And Albigeois and men uncouth,
Folk of the law of devilry,
Who should make our faith deny:
But these the Knighthood have in fear.
Therefore should we hold full dear
In honour and in worship meet,
And ever rise upon our feet
Against their coming from afar.
Certes well worth the shame they are
Who hold such men in grudge and hate.
For now forsooth I tell you straight,
That power full due still hath the Knight
To have his weapons all aright,
And them in holy church to bear
When he hath will the mass to hear:
That missay may no evil one
The worship of the Mary-Son;
Or the all-hallowed sacrament,
From whence is our salvation sent.
And if missayeth and wight,
There may he slay the same outright.

Some deal more needeth yet to say:
Do ye the right, come what come may.
The Knight is bidden hold this same
If he would win the word of fame
This word be must well understand.
Boldly I tell you out of hand

If he after his Order doth
None hinder may, or lief or loth,
But we went straight to Paradise.

*S*o have I learned you this devise
      To do the thing ye should of right
In worship ever of a Knight
Over all men; saving the priest
Who doth the sacrament and feast
Of God's own body. This I tell
True tale that ye may know it well
Of what betided to Prince Hugh,
A valiant man and wise thereto.
Of Saladin great praise had he
Whereas he found his valiancy:
Also be made him honoured fair
Whereas he wrought with pain and care
After his might good works to win.
For good gain lieth still therein,
And in the Latin read I this
Of good dead ever good end is.
So for our ending let us pray
To him who endeth never a day,
That coming to the end of all
We to good ending may befall,
And win unending joyance then
Which hath no end for righteous men.
And pray for him who wrote as well
With Jesus Christ for aye to dwell
And in the love of Mary May.
Now each and all, amen we say.

Chivalry Bookshelf

Publishers of New Works & Important Reprints

Western Martial Arts | Medieval History | Reenactment | Arms & Armour

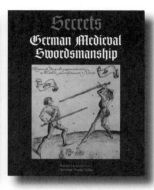

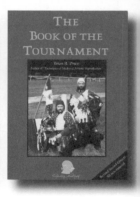

Write for your free catalog or find us online:

http://www.chivalrybookshelf.com

4226 Cambridge Way
Union City, CA 94587 USA
866.268.1495 toll free | 510.471.2944 worldwide |